D0095341

71/12

Every crime was possible to Stalin, for there was not one he had not committed. Whatever standards we use to take his measure, in any event—let us hope for all time to come— to him will fall the glory of being the greatest criminal in history.

Yugoslav dissident Milovan Djilas, 1963

To Mom and Dad, who made so many things possible

Photographs © 2010: AP Images: 59, 86 center, 96, 111; Bridgeman Art Library International Ltd., London/New York: 76 (State Russian Museum, St. Petersburg, Russia); Corbis Images: 88 top (ANSA), 33, 71, 85 top (Bettmann); David King Collection, London: 19, 21, 25, 30, 66, 82 left, 82 right, 84 center, 84 bottom, 85 bottom, 86 bottom, 87 top, 87 bottom, 88 bottom, 88 center, 89 top, 89 bottom, 118; Getty Images: 94 (Keystone), 81 (Alexander Nemenov/AFP), 104 (Pictorial Parade), 55 (Popperfoto), 45 (Slava Katamidze Collection); Library of Congress, George Grantham Bain Collection: 84 top; Sovfoto/Eastfoto: 13, 79; The Granger Collection, New York: 27; The Image Works: 48, 87 center, 114 (akg-images), 89 center (Bilderwelt/US Signal Corps), 109 (Keystone), 86 top (Manchester Daily Express/SSPL), 37, 40, 99 (Mary Evans Picture Library), 61 (Novosti/Topham), 102 (RIA Novosti/TopFoto), 85 center (Topham).

Illustrations by XNR Productions, Inc.: 4, 5, 8, 9
Cover art, page 8 inset by Mark Summers
Chapter art by Raphael Montoliu

Library of Congress Cataloging-in-Publication Data
McCollum, Sean.
Joseph Stalin / Sean McCollum.
p. cm. — (A wicked history)
Includes bibliographical references and index.
ISBN-13: 978-0-531-20755-0 (lib. bdg.) 978-0-531-22355-0 (pbk.)
ISBN-10: 0-531-20755-2 (lib. bdg.) 0-531-22355-8 (pbk.)
1. Stalin, Joseph, 1879–1953—Juvenile literature. 2. Heads of state—Soviet Union—Biography—Juvenile literature. 3. Soviet Union—History—1925–1953—Juvenile literature. I. Title.
DK268.S8M39 2010
947.084'2092—dc22
[B]

200903873

Tod Olson, Series Editor
Marie O'Neill, Art Director
Allicette Torres, Cover Design
SimonSays Design!, Book Design and Production
Thanks to David Brandenberger, University of Richmond

© 2010 Scholastic Inc.

A WICKED HISTORY™
20TH CENTURY

Joseph Stalin

SEAN MCCOLLUM

Franklin Watts®
An Imprint of Scholastic Inc.
New York   Toronto   London   Auckland   Sydney
Mexico City   New Delhi   Hong Kong
Danbury, Connecticut

The World of
JOSEPH STALIN

Under the dictatorship of Joseph Stalin, the Soviet Union rose
from an underdeveloped empire to a global superpower—
at a terrible cost to its people.

Atlantic Ocean

GREAT BRITAIN

miles
0 · 300 · 600

0 · 300 · 600
kilometers

Federal Republic of Germany (West Germany)

German Democratic Republic (East Germany)

Barents Sea

Berlin

LITHUANIA

FINLAND

CZECHOSLOVAKIA

HUNGARY

POLAND

ESTONIA
LATVIA

C St. Petersburg (once Petrograd and Leningrad)

BELORUSSIA

Vinnytsya

D Moscow

Kiev

H

BULGARIA

ROMANIA

UKRAINE

E Poltava

SOV

Ob River

Mediterranean Sea

Black Sea

G Yalta

Volga River

F

Kolpashev

Stalingrad (once Tsaritsyn, now Volgograd)

Caucasus Mtns

Gori

A

Tiflis (now Tbilisi) B

ARMENIA

Caspian Sea

N *Arctic Ocean*

Bering Sea

Pacific Ocean

S i b e r i a

ON

KEY

Joseph Djugashvili (later called Stalin) was born in 1878.

In 1899, Stalin became a revolutionary after he was kicked out of seminary.

Stalin helped the Bolsheviks seize power during the October Revolution of 1917.

Lenin died in 1924, and Stalin began to seize control of the Communist Party.

E Millions of peasants died in 1932–1933 in a famine caused by Stalin's policies.

F In 1943, Soviet troops destroyed an invading German army, marking a major turning point in World War II.

G In 1945, Stalin met with U.S. President Franklin Roosevelt and British Prime Minister Winston Churchill to divide Europe into "spheres of influence."

H Stalin died in his country home in 1953 after suffering a stroke.

Soviet Union as of 1928   Territory added to the Soviet Union by 1947

Nations dominated by the Soviet Union as of 1948   —— Iron Curtain

map is a Lambert Azimuthal equal-area projection, not a Mercator projection.

TABLE OF CONTENTS

A WICKED WEB

A look at the allies and enemies of Joseph Stalin.

Family

~~~~~~~~~~~~

EKATERINA DJUGASHVILI
his mother

BESARION DJUGASHVILI
his father

EKATERINA SVANIDZE
his first wife

NADYA ALLILUYEVA
his second wife

YAKOV
his son with Ekaterina

SVETLANA AND VASILY
his children with Nadya

JOSEPH STALIN

Communist Officials

VLADIMIR LENIN
leader of the Bolshevik Revolution

LEON TROTSKY
Bolshevik leader and
Stalin's main rival

SERGEI KIROV
Leningrad Party leader
and potential rival

NIKOLAI YEZHOV
head of the NKVD,
Stalin's secret police

**GRIGORY ZINOVIEV
AND LEV KAMENEV**
Party leaders purged by Stalin

Other World Leaders

WINSTON CHURCHILL
prime minister of Great Britain,
1940–1945; 1951–1955

FRANKLIN D. ROOSEVELT
president of the United States,
1933–1945

HARRY S. TRUMAN
president of the United States,
1945–1953

ADOLF HITLER
ruler of Nazi Germany,
1933–1945

IN 1979, THE SPRING MELT SWELLED THE waters of the Ob River, which snakes across the frozen tundra of Siberia in central Russia. The rising waters licked away at the river's sandy banks near the town of Kolpashevo.

As the current eroded the riverbanks, it unearthed a secret that had been buried there for decades. Human skeletons began to tumble from the ground. Half-frozen, mummified bodies surfaced in the layer below the skeletons. Many of the remains slid into the river.

The secret police of the Soviet Union—the feared KGB—appeared quickly on the scene. They roped off the area and hurried to make the nightmarish vision disappear. They forced local residents to tie weights to the bodies and sink them in the river. The dead, the KGB claimed, were military deserters executed after World War II.

Although few people believed the story, no one argued with the KGB agents. Sixty years of Communist rule had taught the Soviet people to keep their mouths shut. People who dared to question official stories flirted with arrest—or worse.

But the people of Kolpashevo knew the truth. The local secret police headquarters had once stood above that spot along the broad river. In the late 1930s, friends, relatives, and neighbors had been corralled in mass arrests and led behind the gates of the headquarters. There they were shot in the back of the head and shoveled into a mass grave.

Evidence of the grisly executions lay buried in the riverbanks until that spring of 1979. "In the preserved corpses, some Kolpashevo residents recognized people they knew," journalist Adam Hochschild reported years later, "still wearing the same shoes and clothes they had been arrested in some 40 years earlier."

The dead of Kolpashevo had been consumed in a campaign of terror inspired by a single man: Joseph Stalin.

In his 25 years of rule—from 1928 to 1953—Stalin and the Communist leadership hammered the underdeveloped Soviet Union into an atomic superpower. But they built their empire on the bodies of millions of victims. Some died behind gates like those at Kolpashevo, executed for crimes real or imagined. Others were worked to death in bleak prison camps. Millions more died of starvation in a famine caused by Stalin's cold-blooded policies.

The true story of Stalin's rule, like the secrets of Kolpashevo, lay buried for decades. In recent years it has emerged as one of the greatest tragedies of the twentieth century.

IN 1940, STALIN'S SECRET POLICE EXECUTED 15,000
Polish military officers who had been taken prisoner during
the first months of World War II. German officers discovered
a mass grave filled with thousands of these officers in Katyn
Forest in 1943 (above).

PART 1

BIRTH OF A REVOLUTIONARY

CHAPTER 1

The Toughest Choirboy

Joseph uses his brains and fists to overcome A HARSH CHILDHOOD.

Stalin was born Joseph Djugashvili on December 6, 1878, about a hundred years before the Ob River revealed Kolpashevo's secrets. His parents, Ekaterina (Keke) Djugashvili and Besarion (Beso) Djugashvili, were thrilled by the birth of their third son. They prayed he would live longer than their first two boys, who had died before taking their first steps.

Joseph, or Soso as he was called, had his own near misses while growing up in the small town of Gori. At the age of six he survived a bout with smallpox that left his face scarred with pockmarks. Later, he injured his legs and left arm in a carriage accident, causing him to walk awkwardly for the rest of his life. He remained self-conscious about his appearance even as he grew into a dark-haired young man with piercing brown eyes.

Gori sat in a valley below the Caucasus Mountains of Georgia, a region that had been claimed by Russia in 1801. Its streets were lined with the shops of artisans who crafted furniture, clothing, carpets, and leather goods. They traded their wares for onions, sweet peppers, potatoes, beef, and lamb brought in by peasants from the countryside.

Soso's father worked as a shoemaker in Gori. Beso was an angry man who drank heavily and beat his wife and son. Soso once threw a knife at his father in order to protect his mother from a beating. When the knife missed, Soso had to run for his life.

For most of his childhood Soso found himself at the center of a bitter battle between his parents. Beso could barely make a living as a cobbler, but he was convinced that shoemaking was good enough for his boy. Strong-willed Keke, however, had other ambitions for Soso. She was determined to see him wear the long black robes of a Russian Orthodox priest.

Soso showed enough promise to raise his mother's hopes. He rarely missed mass and sang in a sweet, high voice at church weddings. He had a quick mind and a steel-trap memory, and he got good grades in school. He read greedily, sometimes stealing books from bookshops or classmates.

The talented student also had a wild side. Georgians had a reputation for drinking hard, singing loud, and settling feuds with punches if not daggers. Soso fit right in. He led a gang of rowdy boys in the streets of Gori. He wasn't above fighting dirty if an opponent started to get the better of him. And he seemed to enjoy violence for its own sake.

AS A TEENAGER, Joseph Stalin was a bully,
notorious for acts of violence and vandalism.

When Soso was 12, the tension between his parents erupted into an open battle. Beso had lost his business and taken work in a shoe factory, 45 miles away in the city of Tiflis (later called Tbilisi). On one of his visits to Gori, he insisted that Soso give up his schooling and join him as an apprentice in the factory. Keke argued stubbornly against it. But Beso snatched his son and dragged him to Tiflis.

Keke appealed to Soso's teachers, her priest, and a family friend for help. They came to the rescue, pressuring Beso into surrendering the boy. But Beso vowed never to part with another penny to support the family. Soso returned to Gori with his mother to resume his studies. He rarely saw his father after that.

Three years later, Soso once again made the journey to Tiflis. This time he went willingly. He was 15 and had aced the entrance exams for the Tiflis Spiritual Seminary. The young street brawler was going to become a priest.

THE RUSSIAN EMPIRE

AT THE TIME OF STALIN'S BIRTH, RUSSIA WAS ruled by hereditary emperors known as tsars. Over the previous 100 years, the kings and queens of Western Europe had given up much of their power to parliaments whose members were elected by the people. But the tsars held firm. They still had the power to make laws without consulting anyone.

The tsars ruled a large empire populated mostly by poor and illiterate peasants. But Russian cities were growing fast. New factories drew farmers to urban areas in search of jobs. Many industrial laborers worked 60-hour weeks at unsafe jobs for little pay. They lived in overcrowded barracks and struggled to feed their families.

As their numbers grew, these workers banded together to demand better conditions. They organized strikes and slowly gained power. By the time young Soso left home, some Russians were secretly plotting to overthrow the tsar.

TSAR NICHOLAS II
and his wife, Alexandra,
in 1903

CHAPTER 2

Becoming Koba

Joseph leaves seminary and
EMBRACES REVOLUTION.

Soso's LIFE TOOK A SHARP TURN SHORTLY
after he reached seminary. At first, he did well in his
classes. He wrote poetry and liked to read novels. But
a different, more turbulent kind of life soon drew his
attention away from school.

By the 1890s, young activists had begun to recruit
laborers all across Russia. They held secret meetings in
homes, meeting halls, and bookstores. They encouraged
laborers to form unions and stage protests and strikes to
demand better working conditions.

But for the most radical of the activists, small changes weren't enough. They wanted workers to arm themselves and launch a violent revolution. It was time, they urged, to overthrow the tsar and seize control of the country in the name of the working class.

These were explosive ideas—in Russia and the rest of the world. The most important revolutionary thinker was a German philosopher named Karl Marx, and most of his books had been banned by the tsar. Marxist texts were smuggled into the country and passed secretly from hand to hand.

Soso discovered Marxism in Tiflis. He read all the Marxist books he could get his hands on, sneaking them into the seminary under his clothes. He also slipped out at night to attend secret meetings of railroad workers. Those meetings gave him a chance to see the "workers' struggle" up close.

Fired by his new passion, Soso decided he needed a more appropriate nickname and started to insist that people call him "Koba." He took the name from a ruthless Robin Hood-like character in a popular Georgian novel, a freedom fighter with a taste for revenge. "His face shone with pride and pleasure when we called him 'Koba,'" recalled a fellow student at the seminary.

Koba got himself kicked out of seminary in 1899 after his teachers had caught him reading banned books more than a dozen times. He would never wear the robes of a priest. But the 20-year-old found the life of a professional revolutionary more to his liking. He quickly took to the world of plots, disguises, violence, and life on the run.

Koba joined the country's biggest Marxist group, the Russian Social-Democratic Workers' Party. Working for the party in Georgia, he organized protests, strikes, and riots. At one point, he was suspected of setting a fire in an oil refinery.

The tsar's secret police—known as the *Okhrana*—caught up to Koba in 1902. They sent him into exile in Siberia, a punishment that most revolutionaries

DEBRIS FROM STREET FIGHTING during the Revolution of 1905.
Workers, peasants, and soldiers had rioted across the country to protest
the rule of Tsar Nicholas II.

considered to be a badge of honor. Koba soon escaped
and went back to organizing workers in Tiflis.

In 1905, Koba joined in as a wave of violent
protests threw all of Russia into chaos. Peasants

lashed out at their landlords, burning their estates to the ground and torching police stations. Workers formed councils known as "soviets" to organize strikes and demonstrations. Koba and other revolutionaries created battle squads to harass and kill tsarist troops.

By October, Tsar Nicholas II was forced to compromise with the protesters. He agreed to share power with a parliament, or *Duma*, whose representatives would be elected by the people. At the same time, he dealt ruthlessly with anyone who continued to protest. The tsar allowed vigilante death squads called the Black Hundreds to roam the countryside and crush all signs of public protest.

Nicholas survived the uprising, which became known as the Revolution of 1905. Koba and his fellow revolutionaries had to retreat from public protests and rallies. But they had proven that the tsar's position was shaky. It was only a matter of time before they would strike again.

MARXISM 101

OF THE TEXTS THAT KOBA AND HIS COLLEAGUES secretly passed around, the most important was Karl Marx's *The Communist Manifesto*. To revolutionaries around the world, Marx's skinny pamphlet was a bible. To kings, queens, presidents, and prime ministers, it was perhaps the most dangerous book ever written.

According to Marx, modern society was divided into two groups, or classes. The capitalists owned the businesses, factories, and land, and held most of the power. The laborers, or working class, depended on the capitalists for their livelihood. Capitalists grew wealthy by overworking laborers and keeping the profits for themselves.

When working conditions grew intolerable, Marx predicted, workers would rebel. Eventually, they would crush the capitalists and seize control of their property. They would then set up a communist state run by and for laborers.

"From each according to their ability; to each according to their need," would be the first principle of the new society.

That, at least, was the theory. The reality, as the Russian people would soon find out, was something entirely different.

KARL MARX,
1818–1883

CHAPTER 3

Lenin's Gangster

Koba and his gang fund
LENIN'S SCHEMES,
but the Bolsheviks struggle.

IN NOVEMBER 1905, KOBA TRAVELED IN disguise to Finland for a meeting of communist leaders. There he met the man he called "the mountain eagle"—Vladimir Ilyich Lenin. Lenin was the leader of the Bolsheviks, the most radical wing of the Social-Democratic Party.

Lenin, who had been exiled from Russia, described Koba as "exactly the kind of person I need." He asked Koba to raise money for the Bolsheviks. Lenin and his followers needed funds to print underground newspapers, bribe tsarist officials, and finance assassination squads.

Koba returned to the Caucasus and took up life as a gangster. He and his gang, known simply as "the Outfit," robbed banks, trains, and mail ships. In one murderous assault, Koba's gangsters blew up two horse-drawn carriages carrying bags of cash for a Tiflis bank. By the time the smoke cleared, 40 people were dead and the Bolsheviks were a quarter of a million rubles richer.

The Bolsheviks used cash seized by Koba and others to support a campaign of terrorism against the tsar and his government. They sent squads of assassins armed with rifles, pistols, and homemade bombs into Russian cities. Between 1906 and 1909, the Bolsheviks and other revolutionary groups killed more than 2,600 police and government officials.

Koba stayed active in the movement—when he wasn't stuck in Siberia. Between 1908 and 1913 he was arrested five times and banished to tiny villages in the far north and east of Russia. Each time he escaped, the Okhrana caught up with him and sent him away again.

While stranded in exile, Koba studied Marxism and maintained contact with Lenin and other Bolsheviks by mail. He also took yet another nickname. He published

TSARIST SECRET POLICE took these mug shots of Stalin in 1913. He had already been arrested and sent away for his revolutionary activities five times.

an article and signed it "Stalin"——Russian for "Man of Steel." This time the name stuck.

In 1913, Stalin was arrested yet again, this time in St. Petersburg. He was sentenced to four years of exile. He was locked in a train behind barred windows with other convicted revolutionaries and sent back to Siberia. Eventually, he was taken to Kureika, a frozen village along the Arctic Circle.

While Stalin fished and hunted in exile, a disastrous war was about to engulf all of Europe. Before the fighting was over it would shake the Russian Empire to its foundation and give the Bolsheviks the chance they had been waiting for.

The Russian Revolution

The Bolsheviks seize power
in the midst of
A WORLDWIDE WAR.

IN AUGUST 1914, THE GREATEST ARMIES of Europe marched into the bloody four-year catastrophe known as World War I. For many of the countries involved, the war was pointless; 16 million people were killed and very little was gained.

For Nicholas II, World War I was a fatal disaster.

On the battlefield, the tsar met with one failure after another. He sent his troops to battle the Germans and the Austrians along Russia's western border. For two years the army lost ground—at the cost of nearly 10,000 soldiers a week.

On the home front, the war pushed the Russian people to the breaking point. Every month, thousands of young men were drafted into the army and sent to the battlefront to die. To supply them with weapons and food, the rest of the population paid a fortune in taxes. The cost of basic goods soared. Workers in the cities had little more than porridge and bread to eat.

A PRIEST SPEAKS TO RUSSIAN SOLDIERS wounded during World War I. Russia suffered more casualties during the war than any other country.

After two and a half years of appalling bloodshed, the people's frustration exploded into violence. The Russian Revolution began. In the first phase—known as the February Revolution—workers in the cities rose up in anger.

In the capital of Petrograd (also known as St. Petersburg), women textile workers left their jobs to protest bread shortages. They marched through the city, stopping at factories to pull other workers into the streets.

The striking workers formed the Petrograd Soviet, patterned after the workers' councils formed during the Revolution of 1905. Soon 3,000 delegates were meeting to direct the revolt. Within days, nearly all of the city's factories and shops had been shut down. When the tsar sent army units to break up the strikes, thousands of soldiers mutinied and joined the rebellion.

By the beginning of March, Nicholas II had to admit that he had lost control of his country. He was forced to give up his throne. The tsar was arrested along with the rest of his family. His former subjects danced, sang, and drank vodka in the streets. Almost four centuries of tsarist rule had come to an end.

But the question remained: What would take its place? In the early days after the February Revolution, members of the Duma took control and formed a Provisional Government. The prime minister and most of his top officials were wealthy politicians who had spent many years trying to seize power from the tsar. They wanted democracy but dragged their feet in planning free elections.

The soldiers and workers whose protests had ousted the tsar were dissatisfied. In addition to elections, they wanted higher wages, cheaper goods, and more control over their workplaces. They also wanted Russian troops called home from the front. And their representatives in the Petrograd Soviet demanded a strong role in the new government.

In March, Stalin returned from exile and thrust himself into the middle of the turmoil. Lenin arrived three weeks later and insisted that now was the time to bring communism to Russia. He denounced the Provisional Government and demanded that all power be given to the Petrograd Soviet. Soon the streets were filled with angry crowds chanting the Bolshevik slogan "Peace! Land! Bread!"

Over the next six months, workers, peasants, and soldiers virtually took over the country. Peasants rose up against their landlords, burning homes and seizing land. Workers formed soviets in cities all across Russia and elected Bolsheviks to lead them. In September and October, strikes spread from mines to oil fields, factories, and railroad lines. The strikers were supported by the Red Guards—industrial workers who took up arms to fight for their local soviet councils.

On October 25, 1917, the Russian Revolution entered its final stage—the October Revolution. Lenin, Stalin, and other Bolshevik leaders decided they had become strong enough to seize power. They rallied the Red Guards and took over post offices and telegraph offices in Petrograd.

Just after midnight, the revolutionaries stormed the lightly defended Winter Palace, the seat of the Provisional Government. Fearful officials waited inside a conference room. "I declare all of you ... under arrest," announced the Red Guard commander.

The October Revolution—the world's first successful communist revolt—had been completed with almost no bloodshed at all. The same would not be said for the building of the first communist state.

DURING THE OCTOBER REVOLUTION of 1917, Bolsheviks occupied the Winter Palace.

C H A P T E R   5

Red Alert

The Bolsheviks fight to
IMPOSE COMMUNISM
on the Russian people.

THE OCTOBER REVOLUTION PUT LENIN, Stalin, and the Bolsheviks firmly in charge of Petrograd. But their work was just beginning. They needed to establish control over 180 million people and an area twice the size of the United States. As the Bolsheviks cracked down on their opposition, the Russian people got a bitter taste of their future under communist rule.

By the end of 1917, the Bolsheviks had already made plenty of enemies. Landlords bitterly resented the peasants who now worked the land as if it were their own. Capitalists despised the laborers who had taken over their factories. All across the country, wealthy and middle-class Russians feared for their property—and their lives.

Foreign leaders were equally alarmed by the Bolsheviks. If rough-handed peasants and factory workers were allowed to seize power in Russia, would Great Britain or the United States be next? According to British minister of war Winston Churchill, the Bolshevik Revolution had to be "strangled in its cradle."

With help from Great Britain, France, the U.S., and Japan, anti-Bolshevik groups in Russia organized resistance to the Communists. Joined by thousands of soldiers from the tsar's former army, they formed a loose band of forces known as the White Army.

Lenin, Stalin, and the Bolshevik leadership moved quickly to prepare for civil war. Lenin's commissar for foreign affairs, Leon Trotsky, signed a peace agreement with the Germans and the Austrians and pulled Russia out of World War I. To replace the all-volunteer Red

Guards, Trotsky formed a disciplined new communist force, the Red Army.

As the Red Army began to do battle with the Whites, Lenin imposed communism on the Russian people. He dissolved the parliament and declared that the soviet councils now governed the country. From their new capital in Moscow, the Bolsheviks took over land from monasteries and wealthy landowners. Banks were seized by government managers, and all factories were turned over to the soviets.

LEON TROTSKY (with cane) and Stalin were bitter rivals within the Bolshevik party. Trotsky believed the communist experiment in Russia would fail unless it became a "permanent revolution" that spread to Western Europe and beyond. Stalin criticized Trotsky's ideas as "permanent hopelessness."

Lenin called his new system "war communism"—and it didn't look anything like the worker's paradise described by Karl Marx. The Bolsheviks outlawed strikes and told police to shoot workers who defied the ban. Communist Party workers confiscated surplus crops from peasants to feed the Red Army. Food and other essential goods were all to be controlled and distributed by the government.

To defend the revolution's new policies, Lenin created a ruthless security organization known as the *Cheka*. Its job would be to hunt down all enemies of the working class and even to carry out executions. The Cheka's leaders weren't secretive about their goals or their methods. "Without mercy, without sparing, we will kill our enemies in scores of hundreds," they declared in a Red Army newspaper. "Let them drown themselves in their own blood."

In May 1918, Stalin went on a mission that would reveal the tactics of the new regime in all its brutality. Government food supplies were running dangerously low, and his job was to squeeze more grain from the peasants in the fertile farmlands of the Caucasus. He traveled south from Moscow to Tsaritsyn (which he would later rename Stalingrad) and took command of the military forces in the area.

In Tsaritsyn, Stalin proceeded to terrorize the very people the Bolsheviks claimed as their allies—the peasants. He sent army units to demand grain and other provisions from the dirt-poor farmers. Villages that failed to deliver would be burned to the ground. Anyone who resisted was to be arrested or shot on the spot. "You must be absolutely merciless," he explained to a comrade.

Stalin was equally merciless to the Red Army troops under his command. He racked up huge casualties to secure victories against the Whites. At the first hint of dissent from his officers, he lashed out in fury. Many of the Red Army's commanders had recently served under the tsar, and Stalin was convinced they were traitors. He had dozens of officers shot or locked up on suspicion of sabotaging the war effort.

As the acts of brutality piled up, Lenin and Trotsky grew to mistrust Stalin. But they also admitted that he was essential to the revolution. Although Stalin was hotheaded, dangerous, and stubborn, he got things done. And his use of terror was just an extreme version of official Bolshevik policy. "How can you make a revolution without firing squads?" Lenin said. "If we can't shoot [enemy] saboteurs, what kind of revolution is this? Nothing but talk and a bowl of mush!"

By 1921, Stalin's services on the battlefront were no longer needed. The bulk of the White Army had been defeated.

The people of the former Russian Empire were at peace for the first time in seven years. During that time, their country had been through a great upheaval. Their tsar had been deposed—and then executed by the Bolsheviks in 1918. New leaders had seized power, promising to rule in the interests of the poor.

But many people suspected they had simply exchanged one tyrannical government for another.

CHAPTER 6

Last Testament

With Lenin on his deathbed, Stalin
MANEUVERS FOR POWER.

As THE CIVIL WAR CAME TO AN END, the Bolsheviks backed away from the harsh policies of war communism. Seven years of war had left the people exhausted, starving, and angry. More than three million Russians had died in World War I. Millions more perished in the civil war, and most of the dead were civilians.

Protests broke out around the country and forced the Bolsheviks to act. In March 1921, Lenin approved the New Economic Policy (NEP) to quiet the protesters.

THESE PEASANTS in the Volga region were victims of the severe famine of 1921. Some starving people resorted to cannibalism.

The NEP abolished war communism and permitted small business owners to operate without government control. It allowed peasants to trade surplus grain instead of giving it all to the government. Workers were given shorter hours and paid in cash instead of goods.

Lenin's new policy helped to stabilize Russia (soon to be renamed the Union of Soviet Socialist Republics—USSR). But in the meeting halls of Moscow, a battle was about to begin for control of the Bolshevik party. The outcome of that battle would determine the future of the Soviet Union for decades to come.

In May 1922, Lenin was partially paralyzed by a stroke. Doctors ordered him to rest in his home in a suburb of Moscow, and Stalin helped coordinate his medical care. Lenin tried to run the Party from his sickbed, but he no longer had the last word.

With Lenin's death imminent, other Bolshevik leaders maneuvered for position. The Politburo—the top leadership of the Party—included Stalin, Trotsky, Grigory Zinoviev, Lev Kamenev, and Lenin. Stalin was elected general secretary of the Party, the top office. But Trotsky was widely considered to be Lenin's second-in-command. Unlike Stalin, Trotsky was a powerful speaker and a charismatic leader. And the Bolsheviks considered him a hero for leading the Red Army to victory over the Whites during the civil war.

To fight Trotsky's influence, Stalin began to maneuver behind the scenes. He installed devoted followers at all levels of the Communist Party. He packed the secret police and other Party organizations with people he could trust. He charmed lower officials with his teasing humor and close attention. Comrades' requests were often answered with a written note: "I am ready to help you and receive you."

Most importantly, he made sure that his allies were rewarded for obedience. He arranged housing and distributed gifts. Before long, the Communist Party was filled with people who owed their careers and their livelihoods to Stalin. He and some fellow Party members would soon make good use of their loyalty.

In January 1924, Lenin died after suffering another stroke. Stalin managed the funeral and turned it into a public spectacle. Lenin's body was moved to Moscow's Red Square and put on display. Later, Stalin and some fellow Party members arranged for the corpse to be chemically preserved and exhibited permanently.

But there was one part of Lenin's death that Stalin could not control. All the Bolshevik leaders knew that

BOLSHEVIK LEADERS surround Lenin (front row center) at a 1920
meeting of the Politburo, the Soviet Union's supreme political body.
By 1924, Stalin (circled) had forced rivals Lev Kamenev (right of Lenin)
and Grigory Zinoviev (left of Lenin) out of the Party.

Lenin had written out his final instructions for the Party.
The document had become known as Lenin's Testament.

At a meeting in May, Stalin sat grim-faced while the
Testament was read aloud to the Party's leaders. Lenin
warned that a power struggle following his death could
destroy the revolution. He insisted that there was no
single member of the Party fit to succeed him. Trotsky
was too arrogant. Stalin was too rude. Others were weak
politicians or poor thinkers.

In the end, Lenin recommended that his comrades share power between them. And he called for the removal of Stalin from his position as general secretary. In his place, Lenin said, the Party should appoint someone "more patient, more loyal, more courteous, and more attentive to comrades."

These words could have meant the end of Stalin's career, but thanks to his gang of loyal Party members, he not only survived but thrived. For the next three years, he publicly shared power with the other members of the Politburo. Privately, he schemed to get rid of his main rivals—Trotsky, Zinoviev, and Kamenev. He installed a phone in his desk that allowed him to eavesdrop on their phone calls. He sent secret police to spy on their allies.

In November 1927, Stalin struck. His allies voted Trotsky, Kamenev, and Zinoviev out of the Party. Two years later, Stalin forced Trotsky to leave the country entirely. The warning was clear to friend and foe alike: Anyone who opposed the general secretary risked losing their job—or worse.

PART 2

MAN OF STEEL

CHAPTER 7

The Five-Year Plan

Stalin tries to turn the Soviet Union
into an industrial power—
NO MATTER THE COST.

By 1928, STALIN HAD A FIRM ENOUGH
hold on power to take the country in a radical new
direction. He decided it was time to transform the
Soviet Union from a nation of peasants into a true
industrial power.

For decades, Soviet industry had lagged behind
that of Western countries like Great Britain, Germany,
and France. Peasants made up three-quarters of the
population, and many of them still worked their fields

with horse-drawn plows. Soviet power plants produced a fraction of the electricity generated in the West. Many factories still relied on human muscle instead of modern machines. As a result, the Soviet military lacked modern tanks, aircraft, and warships.

Stalin was convinced that if the Soviet Union did not modernize, it would be an easy target for invasion by the capitalist countries of the West. "We have fallen behind the advanced countries by fifty to a hundred years," he warned. "We must close the gap in ten years. Either we do this or we'll be crushed."

To close the gap, Stalin replaced the NEP with the Soviet Union's first Five-Year Plan. The new plan would once again put the government in control of all parts of the economy. Party workers would run factories, farms, and banks. The central government would set goals for everything the Soviet people produced, from steel to schools.

To support his industrial boom, Stalin needed cash to buy machines and other technology from more advanced countries. To raise the cash, he proposed selling massive amounts of grain overseas.

That was bad news for Soviet peasants. They already struggled to harvest enough surplus food to meet the government's demands. Now they would be forced to produce even more.

To squeeze more food out of the countryside, Stalin completely reorganized the way peasants lived and worked. In 1929, he began to push millions of peasants off their land and onto *kolkhozes*—huge collective farms run by the government. The collectives, Stalin claimed, would allow the Party to manage agricultural production more efficiently. Confining peasants to the *kolkhozes* would also make it easier to police the countryside. Under close supervision by the Party, peasants would have trouble organizing protests or hoarding food.

The government recruited 25,000 industrial workers and sent them into the countryside to oversee the collectivization. But they soon discovered that the

WOMEN THRESH GRAIN on a collective farm. Millions of
Soviet lives were devastated during forced collectivization.

peasants weren't giving in without a fight. Families
slaughtered millions of their precious cattle, sheep, and
horses rather than surrender them to collective farms.
Some villagers took up their shotguns and pitchforks
and attacked the Party workers.

Stalin sent in secret police units to crush the uprisings. The police often singled out the families of defiant peasants and executed them on the spot as a warning to their neighbors. "Don't be afraid to take extreme measures," one Party leader commanded his brigade of enforcers. "Comrade Stalin expects it of you. It's a life-and-death struggle."

Other Communists, though, were horrified by what they were being ordered to do. "I am an old Bolshevik," one secret police officer complained. "I worked in the underground against the tsar and then I fought in the civil war. Did I do all that in order that I should now surround villages with machine guns and order my men to fire into crowds of peasants? Oh, no, no, no!"

CHAPTER 8

Kulaks and Gulags

Stalin clears the countryside of
ALL RESISTANCE.

ALL THROUGH 1929, STALIN'S HENCHMEN worked their way through the countryside, forcing peasants onto collective farms. At the beginning of 1930, they received an order that would make the process even more terrifying. They were to identify peasants who were better off than average—known as *kulaks*—and "eliminate them as a class."

Who exactly were the kulaks? Not even Stalin knew for sure. The Soviets defined them as farmers who used hired labor, ran a grain mill or creamery, or rented equipment to other farmers. But the technical definition mattered little and often changed.

In practice, a kulak was anyone who resisted Stalin's push for collectivization. Farmers accused of hoarding grain were kulaks. Peasants who refused to join a collective were kulaks. People who talked back to a Party worker were kulaks. And for many, the label was a death sentence.

On Stalin's orders, "dekulakization" began in January 1930. The secret police invaded village after village, arresting kulaks and marking them for one of three punishments: execution, deportation, or imprisonment in a work camp. No trial was necessary; the decision of a police commander or Party boss was enough to condemn a peasant to death.

Over the next two years, nearly two million people disappeared from the countryside. Some were killed by village mobs, who were encouraged to attack kulak families. Tens of thousands more were shot by the

PEASANTS LOOK AT POSTERS mocking kulaks—farmers who resisted collectivization. "We must smash the kulaks," Stalin insisted. "We must annihilate them."

secret police. The rest were packed into unheated railcars and shipped like cattle to the far reaches of the Soviet Union.

Hundreds of thousands of these deportees, many of them children, ended up in labor colonies known as the *gulags*. The gulags were slave labor camps, and they expanded quickly under the Five-Year Plan. They housed not only kulaks but murderers, thieves, wealthy businessmen, and former supporters of the tsar. Inmates were forced to chop wood for timber and mine gold. They built roads, canals, and railways. They provided a vast pool of free labor to fuel Stalin's industrial boom.

Prisoners endured hideous conditions inside the gulags. They labored for long hours at backbreaking jobs. They lived on starvation rations and received little medical care. They were purposely worked to exhaustion. They died by the thousands.

Sadistic guards punished prisoners for any reason or no reason at all, sometimes torturing them in gruesome ways. Gulag survivor Alexander Solzhenitsyn described one such torment in his book *The Gulag Archipelago*. A prisoner who had been singled out for bad behavior could be thrown in a dark closet that Solzhenitsyn called a "bedbug infested box." Hundreds of hungry parasites would swarm the miserable victim. "At first," Solzhenitsyn wrote, "he waged war with them strenuously, crushing them on his body and on the walls, suffocated by their stink. But after several hours he weakened and let them drink his blood without a murmur."

Joseph Stalin, who had spent years in the tsar's Siberian prison camps, was now sending his own people to an even worse fate. And he was just getting started.

THE GULAGS

IN 1928, WHEN THE FIVE-YEAR PLAN BEGAN, Soviet labor camps housed about 30,000 prisoners. Over the next 25 years, Stalin would send millions of people to the gulags. People could disappear into the camps for stealing a loaf of bread, failing to show up for work, or telling an anti-government joke. Many were sentenced without trial. At least one million would die in the gulags.

Stalin's prison directors tried to manage the gulags with chilling precision. Dieticians determined how much food a prisoner would need to perform a specific task without starving. In reality, many prisoners lived on a meager ration of rye bread and potatoes.

The gulags were Stalin's great shame. Yet the world knew little about them until the writer Alexander Solzhenitsyn emerged from eight years in a prison camp. His novel *One Day in the Life of Ivan Denisovich* would expose the brutal conditions in the camps. It was first published in 1962, nine years after Stalin's death.

Writer Alexander Solzhenitsyn was in the gulag from 1945 to 1953.

CHAPTER 9

Murder by Starvation

THE FIVE-YEAR PLAN
causes famine in the breadbasket of the Soviet Union.

AT THE END OF 1932, STALIN PROUDLY announced that the Five-Year Plan had been completed a year ahead of schedule. The achievements were astonishing. Factories produced four times as much as they had in 1928. Tractors, tanks, and airplanes rolled off newly constructed assembly lines. Nearly 12 million new laborers had been put to work. Stalin had created an industrial powerhouse, and he had done it in just four years.

The statistics, however, concealed a dark secret. While Stalin exported vast amounts of grain to pay for his new factories, millions of people in the grain-growing heartland of the Soviet Union were starving to death. The Five-Year Plan had created one of the worst famines in human history—right in the middle of the country's most productive farmland.

Stalin had long been suspicious of the peasantry, especially those who occupied the fertile regions of Ukraine, southern Russia, and Kazakhstan. Peasants had stubbornly resisted the Red Army's attempts to draft recruits and seize supplies during the civil war. They had rebelled against the demands of war communism. Now they were standing in the way of Stalin's plan to modernize the Soviet Union.

When collectivization began in 1928, peasants clung stubbornly to their private farms. Stalin fought back with equal persistence——and much greater force. Nearly one million defiant kulaks were deported to gulags in Siberia. Party officials invaded the countryside to seize grain and livestock from private farmers at gunpoint. The officials took not only food but much of the seed needed to sow crops for the coming year.

Pavlo Solodko was ten in 1932, when his family began to feel the strain. His parents had refused to join a collective, and Party workers kept returning to the family's farm to demand higher and higher quotas of grain. "We kept some grain in order for our family to survive the winter," he recalled. "But the brigades were walking around our farms and snooping, and gradually took away everything to the last grain."

In the winter of 1932 to 1933, the first signs of a growing disaster emerged. Officials in the provinces of Kiev and Vinnytsya reported food shortages and hunger on a massive scale. Hospitals were clogged with cases of malnutrition. In the fields, peasants were dropping dead of starvation.

By the spring, a terrible famine had spread across the countryside. People swarmed train stations, hoping to find food in the cities. When they arrived they found no relief. Food was strictly rationed, and lines at government supply stations stretched for blocks.

Peasants resorted to desperate measures to feed themselves and their children. "They caught mice, rats, sparrows, ants, and earthworms," reported the writer Vasily Grossman. "They ground up bones into flour. And when the grass came up, they began to dig up roots and eat the leaves and buds; they used everything there was." When parents could no longer find anything to eat, they left their children on street corners in the hope that someone would take them in and feed them.

Reports of cannibalism leaked out from the worst affected regions. In the city of Poltava, children started mysteriously disappearing from the streets. Before long, fresh supplies of meat appeared in the normally barren city markets. Upon inspection, the meat was found to be human flesh.

TWO FAMINE VICTIMS lie on a sidewalk in Kharkov, Ukraine. Several million people died during Stalin's forced collectivization campaign. Stalin called stories of the peasants' suffering "fables."

As people struggled to survive, they found that they had few options. Stalin closed Ukraine's borders in January 1933, so no one could flee in search of food. He also made sure that theft was not an option. By Stalin's own decree, anyone caught stealing so much as five ears of corn from a collective could be put to death. His agents even inspected people's feces for signs that they were illegally consuming grain.

Even at the cost of millions of lives, Stalin was determined to stick to his economic plan. In the midst of the famine, precious food flowed out of the Soviet Union by the shipload. Village dairies in Ukraine churned butter and packed it for export while starving people waited in bread lines down the street. In 1932 and 1933, the worst years of the famine, the Soviet Union collected nearly 30 million tons of grain from peasants and sold it overseas.

By end of 1933, the Soviet countryside had been devastated. Once-lively villages had become ghost towns with skeleton-thin corpses lining the streets. At least three million people had died of starvation and disease. Millions more suffered in the gulags, in Siberian exile, or on collective farms.

In Stalin's time, few people understood the extent of the disaster. Stalin banned journalists and other writers from publishing accounts of the famine.

Today, Ukrainians remember the famine as the *Holodomor*, or "murder by starvation." Many people believe that Stalin not only allowed it to happen but deliberately caused the disaster in order to wipe out Ukrainian resistance to Communist rule.

CHAPTER 10

The Red Tsar

From inside the Kremlin, Stalin builds a CULT OF PERSONALITY.

Sᴛᴀʟɪɴ ᴀɴᴅ ᴏᴛʜᴇʀ ᴍᴇᴍʙᴇʀs ᴏꜰ ᴛʜᴇ Politburo rarely traveled to the countryside to face the harsh consequences of their decisions. They ruled from their headquarters inside the Kremlin, a fortress in the heart of Moscow.

Soviet leaders kept apartments in the Kremlin's Poteshny Palace, a short walk from their offices. Almost daily, they dropped by each other's homes for a visit.

They ate dinner and went to movies together. On days off, they took family trips to their *dachas*, or country homes. They even vacationed together at resorts along the Black Sea coast.

In the early 1930s, Stalin and his fellow Politburo members resembled a big family—a mob family. Stalin, the Party's general secretary, was the big boss. He was an extremely hard worker who demanded the same dedication from the rest of his circle. On a typical day he rose in the late morning and worked his way through stacks of government papers, puffing on his pipe and marking decisions in red and blue pencil. He rarely dressed in anything fancier than his usual military-style shirt, riding pants, and soft leather boots.

In the mid-afternoon, Stalin often had a big meal with family and friends. The gathering of comrades usually included his wife, Nadya, and their two children, Vasily and Svetlana, as well as Yakov, his son from his first marriage. Stalin enjoyed horsing around with the kids. On occasion he would wad up balls of bread to toss at companions or plunk into their drinks. After the late lunch and perhaps a nap, he returned to the office to continue his work late into the night.

While he lived a relatively ordinary life in private, a different, almost superhuman image of Stalin was growing beyond the Kremlin walls. Official propaganda constantly reminded the Soviet people of Stalin's supposedly tireless devotion to the country. His picture often appeared on the front page of the official Soviet newspaper, *Pravda*, as he presented medals to the hardest-working miners or milkmaids. "Stalin's life is our life, our beautiful present and future," *Pravda* proclaimed. Kids in the Young Pioneers—the Soviet version of the Girl Scouts and Boy Scouts—appeared on posters above the slogan, "Thank you, Comrade Stalin, for our happy childhood."

The Party tightly controlled the way its leader was portrayed in the media. Cartoons of Stalin were forbidden in newspapers and magazines. Instead, paintings and photos showed him looking wisely into the distance, as if planning the nation's future. He always appeared in simple clothes to make himself look like a man of the people.

Stalin was building a "cult of personality"—a heroic public image that encouraged people to idolize him without thinking critically about his policies. This hero worship served an important purpose. First of all, it

GOVERNMENT PROPAGANDA portrayed Stalin as a wise and caring leader. Here, he autographs photos for two visitors from a collective farm during their visit to Moscow in 1935.

kept Stalin in power. To many people, "Comrade Stalin" *was* the Soviet revolution. Without him, they believed, the nation would fall apart. Stalin's cult of personality also bound the Soviet people to the state. Citizens who revered their leader were more likely to remain loyal to the government and follow its policies without objection.

Publicly, Stalin liked to be seen as a humble leader. But he understood all too well the value of being worshipped like a god.

In 1935, Stalin, his children, and some friends paid a surprise visit to the newly opened Metro, Moscow's subway. Surprised commuters pressed in to get a glimpse of their leader and shout compliments.

Afterward, he described how much he had enjoyed the outing. He was inspired by the spontaneous "love of the people for their leader," he told a friend. "The people need a tsar, whom they can worship and for whom they can live and work."

The man who had helped to overthrow the last tsar now claimed that role for himself.

CHAPTER 11

A Mysterious Murder

The assassination of Kirov
OPENS THE GATE TO TERROR.

IN JANUARY 1934, COMMUNIST PARTY delegates descended on Moscow from all parts of the Soviet Union. They made the journey every few years to elect the Party's Central Committee and discuss plans with each other. Many arrived in colorful clothing that highlighted the diversity of the Soviet people. The gathering included Cossacks outfitted in their long *cherkesska* coats, Kazakhs topped with fox fur hats, and Uzbeks wearing tight turbans and gold-embroidered kaftans.

In speech after speech at the Party Congress, Communist leaders boasted about the "victories" won since the beginning of the Five-Year Plan. "Our successes are really tremendous," gushed Politburo member Sergei Kirov. "Damn it all . . . you just want to live and live—really, just look what's going on. It's a fact!" Stalin joined in the booming applause.

But as the Central Committee election approached, Stalin was no longer clapping. Despite their public show of unity, regional Party leaders were tired of Stalin's extreme measures. They had spent five years confiscating grain and forcing peasants into collectives. They were despised by their own people—and some blamed Stalin.

In the end, Stalin was easily re-elected to his position at the head of the Party. But he knew that there was opposition in the ranks. Delegates were complaining privately about his dictatorial hold on the Party. And some regional leaders were begging for a break from the harsh demands of the Five-Year Plan.

In response, Stalin grumbled that "counter-revolutionaries"—people who opposed the results of the Communist revolution—were endangering the Party. Then he sat back and planned his revenge.

On December 1, 1934, Stalin got the excuse he needed to lash out at his enemies. Sergei Kirov, the most powerful Party leader next to Stalin, was shot dead in Leningrad by an assassin.

Some Party members suspected that Stalin had ordered Kirov's murder to get rid of a dangerous rival. Stalin ignored the rumors and used the incident to cast suspicion on anyone he did not like or trust. "To me it's already clear that a well-organized counter-revolutionary terrorist organization is active in Leningrad [formerly Petrograd]," Stalin announced. "A painstaking investigation must be made."

Less than a week after Kirov's death, Stalin had set his plan in motion. His old adversaries Zinoviev and

Kamenev were arrested and accused of masterminding the plot to kill Kirov. Within a month, they were sentenced to long prison terms, along with several of their sympathizers. Stalin also turned his secret police force loose in Leningrad. Thousands of suspected "counter-revolutionaries" were rounded up and expelled from the city.

Stalin had just fired the opening shots in a ruthless new battle against anyone who threatened his control over the country.

THIS PAINTING SHOWS a somber Stalin standing next to the coffin of Sergei Kirov. Many historians believe that Stalin ordered the murder of his rival.

CHAPTER 12

The Great Terror

Stalin turns the
SECRET POLICE LOOSE
on the Soviet people.

IN 1936, STALIN BEGAN AN ALL-OUT WAR to eliminate anyone who resisted his plans for the Soviet Union. His campaign of terror reached into every corner of the country. It targeted army officers and church leaders, Party officials and peasants.

Stalin's paranoid attack on all forms of dissent became known as the Great Terror. By the time it was over, few people dared to question the dictatorship of the "Man of Steel."

During the Great Terror, Stalin relied on his notorious secret police to do what he called the "black work." The organization's official title was the People's Commissariat for Internal Affairs, but it was better known by its Russian initials NKVD. The NKVD arrested suspects and interrogated them endlessly. Agents often tortured their prisoners into confessing and naming other suspects. Three-person NKVD commissions known as *troikas* had the power to convict prisoners and sentence them to death. NKVD guards then took care of the executions—typically, with a bullet to the back of the head.

In August 1936, Stalin turned the NKVD loose on two of his oldest rivals. He had his agents retrieve Zinoviev and Kamenev from the labor camps. He promised not to harm the two prisoners or their families, as long as they confessed to planning Kirov's assassination.

Zinoviev and Kamenev were given a show trial—a rigged hearing designed to make a public example of

STALIN'S SHOW TRIAL WORKED. Here, factory workers vote in favor of a resolution condemning Stalin adversaries Zinoviev and Kamenev. Similar resolutions were passed in thousands of other factories.

the defendants. The two prisoners did as they were told and gave their confessions. But despite Stalin's promise, they were sentenced to death.

Early the next morning, Zinoviev and Kamenev were dragged from their cells and shot. Afterward, the bullets were removed from their brains and kept by NKVD chief Genrich Yagoda as souvenirs. Stalin also had Kamenev's wife and two sons executed.

In September, Stalin prepared to expand the purge by placing Nikolai Yezhov in charge of the NKVD. A short, cruel man, Yezhov became the chief organizer of the arrests, the trials, and the executions.

Then Stalin announced that the Soviet Union was "encircled by hostile powers" plotting to destroy the revolution. People who had worked for the tsarist government two decades earlier were targeted for arrest. Kulaks who had returned from labor camps were to be hunted down. Anyone who had once joined a political party other than the Communist Party was also at risk.

An atmosphere of fear spread through Party offices, workplaces, and even the homes of ordinary citizens. Party members were encouraged to turn in anyone suspected of anti-Communist thoughts. Husbands and wives accused each other. Children were hailed as heroes for turning in mothers and fathers.

In every region of the country, officials were given quotas for arrests and executions. When local NKVD units met their goals, they sometimes asked permission to arrest more. The NKVD in Stalinabad, for example, was ordered to execute 6,277 people—but ended up shooting more than 13,000. Mass graves were dug outside of towns and cities, filled with bodies, and then bulldozed over.

One of Stalin's main targets was the Soviet military, the last organization that could possibly threaten his grip on power. Stalin accused Red Army officers of secretly collaborating with foreign powers. Then he began arresting and executing his most experienced officers. By the time he was done, he had purged more than three-quarters of his generals, field commanders, and naval admirals. It was a reckless move that would come at an incalculable price.

MEMBERS OF a human-rights group excavate a mass grave near St. Petersburg. In 2002, the group discovered the remains of 30,000 victims of Stalin's purges.

In mid-1938, Stalin slowed down his gory witch hunt. The purges were taking their toll on the Soviet economy. Too many productive workers in agriculture, mining, manufacturing, and government had simply disappeared from their jobs.

But Stalin accomplished what he had set out to do. In two years, he had erased almost everyone who could challenge his one-man dictatorship and terrorized those who survived. In 1940, an assassin even succeeded in killing Leon Trotsky, who had ended up in Mexico City after Stalin forced him into exile in 1929. Trotsky died from a blow to the head with an ice pick.

The scale of the Great Terror was staggering. At least 1.7 million Soviet citizens had been torn from their homes and imprisoned. More than 700,000 of those prisoners ended up in mass graves. The rest spent years of their lives wasting away in the gulags.

As the arrests dwindled, the Soviet people got a brief rest. But it wasn't long before they were dragged into the most destructive war in history.

Stalin with Yezhov   . . . and without him

ERASED FROM HISTORY

AFTER THE GREAT TERROR HAD SERVED HIS purpose, Stalin turned on the very people he had ordered to do his "black work." In April 1939, he had the commissar of the NKVD, Nikolai Yezhov, arrested and jailed. Yezhov was blamed for the excesses of the purge. He was stripped, beaten, dragged sobbing from his cell, and shot. His body was cremated, and the ashes were dumped in a common grave. His death was kept secret for years.

Stalin tried to erase not only Yezhov's life, but his memory as well. It became Soviet tradition to delete all evidence of people who had fallen out of favor. Friends and family members were often executed or exiled to labor camps. Officials altered records and rewrote histories to remove names. They even retouched photos to erase the victims.

That was the fate of Yezhov—one of Stalin's deadliest butchers.

JOSEPH STALIN IN PICTURES

PEACE, LAND, BREAD

A NATION OF PEASANT
When Stalin was born, most Russians were poor and illiterate peasants. They eked out meager livings on small farms.

THE LAST EMPEROR
Tsar Nicholas II and his wife, Alexandra, in 1903. He was all-powerful, but revolution was brewing.

GANGSTER
As a young man, Stalin was a violent revolutionary who robbed banks, trains, and mail ships to raise money for the radical Bolsheviks.

REVOLUTION

In 1917, the Bolsheviks seized power in Russia after the fall of the tsar. Led by Vladimir Lenin, they began to build the world's first communist state.

HAMMER AND SICKLE

This Bolshevik emblem represented unity between factory workers and peasants. The hammer represented workers; the sickle symbolized peasants.

CIVIL WAR BREAKS OUT

Leon Trotsky (below left) led the Bolshevik Red Army in the civil war against the anti-Bolshevik White Army. Stalin was one of Trotsky's most brutal commanders.

SLAVE CAMPS AND FAMINE

POWER STRUGGLE
Lenin (left) and Stalin. After Lenin died in 1924, Stalin vied with rivals for power. By 1927, he was the country's undisputed leader.

KULAKS
Peasants look at a poster depicting kulaks as pigs. Farmers who resisted collectivization were labeled kulaks.

RULE BY TERROR
Stalin's secret police crushed any dissent. Here, they arrest suspects on a Moscow street in 1928.

STALIN'S SLAVE CAMPS

Prisoners building a canal in 1933. Stalin sent millions of people to slave labor camps called *gulags*. Many were worked to death.

WIDESPREAD FAMINE

Stalin's policies created one of the worst famines in history. In the Soviet Union's richest farmland, millions starved to death.

PILES OF GRAIN

During the famine, farmers harvested enough grain to feed the starving population. But Stalin insisted on exporting part of it to pay for his new factories.

STALIN TIGHTENS HIS GRIP

PROPAGANDA

The state-run media portrayed Stalin as a wise and caring leader. Newspaper articles proclaimed him responsible for the Soviet Union's "beautiful present and future."

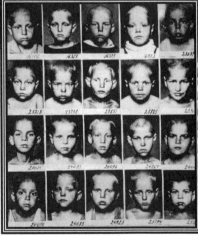

ORPHANED

During the Great Terror, children of Stalin's victims—such as these— were given new names so they could not track down their parents.

DAILY NEWS FINAL

TROTSKY IS DEAD

↑Trotsky Death Weapon

←Dying, He Blamed Stalin

DEATH OF TROTSKY

Exiled in Mexico, Trotsky continued to oppose Stalin from afar. But Stalin had a long reach. In 1940, one of his agents killed Trotsky with an ice pick.

WORLD WAR II
For six months, Red Army soldiers fought to save Stalingrad from the Germans. The USSR suffered 26 million deaths during the war.

UNEASY ALLIES
In 1945, Stalin met with British Prime Minister Churchill (left) and U.S. President Roosevelt (center). With troops throughout Eastern Europe, Stalin was more powerful than ever.

STALIN DIES
Joseph Stalin died in 1953. His regime was one of the bloodiest in history.

PART 3

TRIUMPH AND DECLINE

CHAPTER 13

Pact Between Tyrants

As war clouds gather over Europe,
Stalin cuts a DEAL
WITH ADOLF HITLER.

BY 1939, A VERY REAL THREAT TO STALIN'S
reign had risen in Central Europe. Adolf Hitler, Nazi
Germany's *führer*, or leader, was building a fearsome
war machine—a massive force of modern tanks and
fast-flying dive bombers. It seemed only a matter of
time before he turned them loose on his neighbors.

Hitler had made no secret of his desire to conquer Eastern Europe, including much of the Soviet Union. He had repeatedly declared that the Germans needed more land—and that they would eventually move east to get it. He also hated communism and viewed Russians and other Slavs as an inferior race.

But to Stalin's surprise, he received a letter from Hitler in August 1939. The Nazi führer was proposing an alliance between Germany and the USSR. Hitler intended to attack France and the other nations of Western Europe. To ensure his success, he wanted to avoid going to war on his eastern border while fighting in the west. He suggested that Germany and the Soviet Union agree not to attack each other for ten years.

The German proposal appealed to Stalin. He knew that the Red Army was not yet prepared to fight Hitler's swift and powerful attack force. Stalin also saw a chance to add territory to his own empire. In negotiations, the Germans made it clear that they had plans to attack

Poland. They would be willing to divide any conquered territory with the Soviets.

The German-Soviet treaty was signed on August 23, 1939. Stalin toasted the agreement with vodka. "I know how much the German nation loves its führer," he declared. "He's a good chap. I'd like to drink to his health."

ON AUGUST 23, 1939, Germany and the USSR signed a pact agreeing not to attack each other. Stalin (in light color jacket) watches as his foreign minister, Vyacheslav Molotov, signs the treaty.

The following week, on September 1, German forces crashed into Poland from the west. On September 17, the Red Army pushed in from the east. Within weeks, Poland ceased to exist as a country.

France and Great Britain responded by declaring war on Germany. World War II had begun.

Stalin immediately moved to extend his new gains. In October 1939, the Baltic countries of Estonia, Latvia, and Lithuania were pressured into accepting thousands of Soviet troops.

In late November, the Red Army attacked Finland. Stalin's generals expected an easy victory. The gutsy Finns had other ideas. Though greatly outnumbered and outgunned, Finnish soldiers gave the Red Army all the combat it could handle. It took four months for the Soviets to force Finland into negotiations and to surrender some of its territory. Finland lost 48,000 soldiers, the Red Army more than 125,000.

The struggle in Finland revealed a big weakness in the Soviet military. Factories were producing the

DEAD SOVIET SOLDIERS LIE FROZEN in the snow after a battle in Finland in December 1939. They are surrounded by equipment left behind by fleeing Soviet troops.

tanks, aircraft, and artillery the army needed to fight a major war. But the leadership of the armed forces was a mess. Most of the Red Army's senior officers had been dismissed or executed during Stalin's purges.

Several hundred miles to the west, Adolf Hitler followed the war in Finland with interest. And he did not fail to notice the weakness of Stalin's army.

CHAPTER 14

The Great Patriotic War

The German *blitzkrieg*
extends into the
SOVIET UNION.

IN THE SPRING OF 1940, HITLER LAUNCHED his long-feared invasion of Western Europe. German troops landed in Denmark and Norway in April 1940. A month later, German tanks and dive bombers raced through Belgium to strike the Netherlands and France. This was Germany's *blitzkrieg*, or "lightning war." The strategy relied on speed and overwhelming force to shatter the ranks of its enemies.

The results were stunning. Within two months, virtually all of Western Europe fell before the Nazi onslaught. Only a battered Great Britain held on, bracing for an invasion across the English Channel from Nazi-occupied France.

Stalin watched with apprehension as the Germans carved up the armies of Western Europe. He knew it was only a matter of time before Hitler looked eastward again. But when it finally happened, the Germans caught Stalin unprepared.

In June 1941, military intelligence began warning Stalin that German units were massing along the Soviet border. Stalin refused to believe that they would attack before Great Britain had surrendered.

Stalin ignored all warnings and refused to put the Red Army on highest alert. He did not want to do anything to increase tensions with the Germans.

The German leader, however, did not need an excuse.

On June 22, 1941, Hitler launched Operation Barbarossa—the invasion of the Soviet Union. German aircraft struck deep inside the USSR. The blitzkrieg tore huge gaps in the Red Army's defenses. German infantry and tanks sped across Ukraine and western Russia. They took aim at Kiev, Moscow, and Leningrad. Hundreds of thousands of Red Army soldiers were cut off and captured.

Some Soviet citizens were ready to welcome the Germans as liberators from Stalin's dictatorship. They were never given the chance. German troops brutalized both soldiers and civilians in captured territory. Special

IN JUNE 1941, thousands of German tanks poured into the Soviet Union. By October, they were closing in on Moscow.

units trailed the German army to massacre Jews, Roma, and other groups. Eventually six million Jews would perish in the Holocaust, Hitler's systematic murder of Europe's Jews. Over two million of the victims were killed on Soviet territory.

Within a month, German troops had pushed the Soviet Union to the brink of defeat. The Red Army had already lost two million men, 3,500 tanks, and more than 6,000 aircraft. The German air force was dropping bombs on Moscow by the end of July. The German army surrounded Leningrad on September 9 and captured Kiev ten days later.

With catastrophe looming, Soviet citizens rallied to defend their homelands. Workers disassembled entire factories and shipped them 1,000 miles east to the remote Ural Mountains. Collective farm workers destroyed crops rather than let them fall into German hands. Laborers put in longer hours on assembly lines and produced tanks, planes, and guns by the thousands.

Stalin did what he could to encourage the new patriotic spirit. He relaxed censorship rules. He replaced Communist Party slogans and propaganda with appeals to rescue Mother Russia. The war itself became known as the Great Patriotic War.

But while Stalin used a carrot to motivate civilians, he reserved the stick for his soldiers. Red Army officers received orders to execute deserters and troops who fled from battle. More than 150,000 soldiers were shot in 1941 and 1942 alone. Red Army troops learned to fight to the bitter end, out of fear if not courage.

In October 1941, German tanks closed in on Moscow for what Hitler insisted would be "the last, great decisive battle of the war." Stalin, however, decided to make a stand. He ordered most Party members to evacuate the city. The bulk of the civilian population either fled or enlisted in the army. Even Lenin's embalmed corpse was carted away to the Ural Mountains.

Stalin himself stayed in Moscow and made sure that his decision was heavily publicized. "Pass on to your

NAZI TROOPS execute two Soviets in October 1941. The victims may have been Soviet partisans, civilians who fought against the Nazis.

comrades that they should take their spades and dig their own graves," he told an army commissar. "We . . . are not leaving Moscow."

Stalin's gamble paid off. The Red Army fought fiercely in the suburbs of Moscow and held the Germans off until winter arrived. When the snows finally came, the German invasion froze in place. Weapons and tanks failed in the frigid cold. Supplies ran low as transport vehicles stalled on snowbound roads. When spring came, the people of Moscow and Leningrad were starving, but they still refused to surrender.

Stalin also had a powerful new ally: the United States. The Americans had entered the war after Japan, Germany's ally, attacked Pearl Harbor in December 1941. Stalin had always considered the capitalist U.S. to be one of the Soviet Union's most bitter enemies. But now he eagerly accepted the U.S. as a partner in the fight against Germany. Together with Great Britain and other countries, they formed a powerful alliance known as the Allies.

In June 1942, Hitler ordered a new assault, this time on the city of Stalingrad. German forces surged into the city but could not capture it. The buildings were blasted to rubble, and hundreds of thousands of soldiers and civilians died in one of the deadliest battles in history. Hitler demanded his men take the city or die trying.

Most died trying. In November 1942 the Red Army launched a bold counterattack code-named Operation

Uranus. Within four days, the Soviets had encircled some 330,000 enemy troops. They blocked the enemy's supply lines and fought the Germans street to street, building to building. On February 2, 1943, the top German general finally surrendered. The last 90,000 of his freezing, starving men were captured.

The Red Army had finally begun to dismantle Hitler's war machine.

RED ARMY SOLDIERS defeated the Germans at Stalingrad in February 1943, after six months of brutal fighting. Only 5,000 Germans who attacked Stalingrad survived the war to return to Germany.

CHAPTER 15

Warlord Triumphant

The Allies defeat the Nazis, and
Stalin EXPANDS HIS EMPIRE.

IN NOVEMBER 1943, STALIN MET WITH U.S.
President Franklin D. Roosevelt and British Prime
Minister Winston Churchill in the Iranian capital of
Tehran to discuss the progress of the war.

The fighting was far from over, but the Allies had
the Germans on the defensive. The Red Army was
driving Hitler's troops out of the Soviet Union. The

Americans controlled the Atlantic Ocean. A combined American and British force had landed in Italy and was battling its way north.

Since 1941, Stalin had been impatiently urging Churchill and Roosevelt to launch an invasion of France. A major assault there would force Hitler to fight on a second front. He would have to pull troops out of the Soviet Union to defend the German homeland.

Stalin got his wish, but not right away. On June 6, 1944—a date that became known as D-Day—a vast fleet of troop transports crossed the English Channel. More than 160,000 Allied soldiers landed on the French coast and began fighting their way inland.

Stalin was not impressed. By now he firmly believed that the Soviets would defeat the Nazis with or without a second front. Stalin was convinced that the Americans and the British had delayed the invasion in order to weaken the Soviet army.

Whether his accusation was justified or not, Stalin was right about one thing: The Allies had become rivals.

And the war to defeat Germany had become a race for territory. The Soviets were now charging through Eastern Europe and closing in on Germany from the east. The British, Canadians, and Americans had retaken France and were pressing in from the west. Whoever occupied a country when the Germans surrendered would have tremendous influence there after the war.

The Allied leaders met again in February 1945, in the Ukrainian city of Yalta. Stalin now insisted on a Soviet "sphere of influence" in territories occupied by the Red Army. His aim was to install governments obedient to the Soviet Union in Poland, Estonia, Latvia, Lithuania, Bulgaria, Czechoslovakia, Hungary, and Romania.

Churchill and Roosevelt reluctantly agreed. There was little they could do to oppose Stalin in countries controlled by the Red Army. To free Eastern Europe from Soviet control would have required yet another war. They didn't have the stomach for more combat after six years of the most destructive conflict in human history.

The Red Army captured Berlin in the early days of May 1945. Soviet troops found Hitler's charred corpse outside the bunker where he had spent the final days of the war.

The Soviet people joyously celebrated Hitler's death and their victory. Their country had suffered more casualties than any other during the war. The German invasion had left 26 million Soviets dead, 26 million homeless, and millions more wounded.

There was reason to hope that the people would be rewarded for their sacrifice. Stalin had given them more freedom during the war years. And hadn't his people risen to the challenge and saved the country? The people of Leningrad, for instance, had suffered through a 900-day siege in which one million civilians lost their lives. In a sense, the Soviet people had rescued the dictator himself.

Stalin gave a patronizing thanks to everyone who had sacrificed for the war effort. "I offer a toast to those simple, ordinary, modest people," he said, "to the 'little cogs' who keep our great state mechanism in an active condition in all fields of science, economy, and military affairs."

But there would be no gentler future for Stalin's "little cogs." The NKVD thugs were still doing their "black work"—and now they had all of Eastern Europe to police.

ON MAY 1, 1945, Red Army soldiers raise the Soviet flag on top of the German parliament building in Berlin. A week later, the war in Europe was over.

CHAPTER 16

The Cold War Begins

FORMER ALLIES BECOME RIVALS as Stalin imposes communist rule on Eastern Europe.

THE ALLIED LEADERS MET FOR A FINAL time in July 1945, in Potsdam, Germany. President Roosevelt had died in April. He was succeeded by his vice president, Harry S. Truman.

At Potsdam, Truman tracked down Stalin for a private word. The United States, Truman said, had developed a "new weapon of unusual destructive force."

Stalin acted pleased but asked no questions. In fact, Soviet spies had already informed him of the Americans' successful test of an atomic bomb. Stalin's own top-secret nuclear program was well underway.

Soon after the conference, the U.S. dropped two of its atomic bombs on the Japanese cities of Hiroshima and Nagasaki. The devastating explosions helped force the Japanese to surrender. They also sent a warning to Stalin: *We have the bomb and you don't. Watch your step.*

AN OBSERVER STANDS in the ruins left by the atomic bomb that the U.S. dropped on Hiroshima, Japan, on August 6, 1945.

The threat, however, did not stop Stalin from taking over Eastern Europe. The war had left the entire region in Stalin's hands. As soon as the fighting stopped, the Soviets went to work installing friendly governments in Poland, Czechoslovakia, Hungary, Romania, Albania, and the eastern half of Germany. Latvia, Lithuania, and Estonia were simply absorbed into the USSR.

In these so-called "satellite" states, Stalin set up governments that would do his bidding. Opposition leaders were jailed and killed. Elections were rigged and pro-Soviet leaders put in charge. Private property and businesses were all taken over by the government. The Red Army and secret police stood by, waiting to crush any sign of resistance.

In March 1946, Winston Churchill lashed out at Stalin in a speech that would be quoted for years to come. The countries of Eastern Europe might remain independent in name, he said. But in reality, an "iron curtain has descended across the continent." Eastern Europe was being absorbed into Stalin's empire.

World War II had ended, but a new era of global tension had taken its place. This conflict became known as the Cold War, and it pitted the U.S. and other capitalist democracies against the Soviet Union and the communist governments it controlled. The two superpowers never went to war directly. But they competed viciously for allies around the globe. They sent spies to rival capitals to dig up top-secret information. And they competed in an arms race that would eventually produce enough nuclear weaponry to destroy the world many times over.

In 1948, Stalin challenged the Americans in the first major conflict of the Cold War. After World War II, the Soviets and the other Allies had split Germany between east and west. Berlin sat in the Soviet region. But the city was divided into four zones controlled by the U.S., the USSR, Great Britain, and France.

On June 24, Stalin ordered a blockade set up around the western part of Berlin—the zones controlled by the U.S., Britain, and France. All supplies entering the zones were to be seized. Stalin hoped to force the Western powers to hand over their sections of Berlin. His old allies, he thought, would not dare risk a war by breaking through the blockade.

Stalin was right: The Western powers did not directly challenge the Soviet blockade. Instead, they flew over it in a massive airlift. Flying day and night, cargo planes delivered tons of food and supplies to the trapped people of West Berlin.

After almost 11 months of the Berlin Airlift, Stalin realized that his plan had failed. He called off the blockade. But it was only the beginning of a global conflict that would last for more than four decades.

CHILDREN WATCH a cargo plane fly over Berlin, Germany. The U.S. and other countries dropped food and supplies to the western part of the city, which the Soviets had blockaded.

CHAPTER 17

Final Plots

As his health fails, STALIN KEEPS SCHEMING to stay in control.

THE CONSTANT STRESS OF WORLD WAR II had taken its toll on Stalin, who turned 70 in 1948. Official portraitists did their best to maintain his steely-eyed public image. But his graying hair, stooped shoulders, and stumbling step betrayed his worsening health.

Stalin sometimes claimed he was ready to retire, but it was only a cruel joke. He had no intention of giving up power. He kept a suspicious eye on other Politburo members. He had their phones tapped and rooms bugged. He was determined not to let the smallest threat go undetected.

In the early 1950s, Stalin's paranoia found a new target: Soviet Jews. For years, Stalin had made anti-Semitic comments in private. Many people thought that Jews had been specially targeted during the purges of the 1930s. After the war, Stalin feared that the Jewish people felt allegiance to the United States. "Every Jew is a potential spy," he supposedly warned an associate.

In 1952, Stalin dreamed up an imaginary conspiracy called the Doctors' Plot. Several Party leaders had recently died while in the care of Jewish doctors. Stalin had jailed his own doctor when the man suggested that he retire. On this flimsy evidence, Stalin decided that medical workers around the country had been paid by the United States to poison the Soviet leadership.

Stalin revealed his suspicions at a meeting of Party leaders in December 1952. "You're like blind kittens," he told the other delegates. "What will happen without me? The country will perish because you do not know how to recognize your enemies."

The following month, *Pravda* announced the plot to the public in an editorial titled "Evil Spies and Murderers Masked as Medical Professors." NKVD agents immediately went to work. Hundreds of doctors and medical workers—mostly Jews—were arrested and prepared for trial. People began to whisper that Stalin was preparing to deport all Soviet Jews to Siberia.

But Stalin's final crime collapsed in the early morning hours of March 1. A messenger discovered the dictator on the floor of his country estate, paralyzed after a stroke. He drifted in and out of consciousness for several days but did not speak again.

Joseph Stalin breathed his last breath on March 5, 1953. Perhaps expert medical treatment could have saved him. But the best doctors in Moscow were all in jail.

AFTER HIS DEATH on March 5, 1953, Stalin's body was
put on display for three days. Huge crowds came to see
him, and many people were trampled underfoot.

~~~~~~~~~~~~~~~~~

Epilogue

~~~~~~~~~~~~~~~~~

In 1956, Stalin's successor, Nikita Khrushchev, stunned the delegates of the 20th Congress of the Communist Party. In a secret session, he accused Stalin of murdering thousands of faithful Party members. He went on to charge that Stalin had ignored the teachings of Lenin and built a cult of personality that betrayed the ideals of communism.

The speech left the delegates in a state of shock. For three decades, words like Khrushchev's would have meant a death sentence to anyone foolish enough to utter them. Now, it seemed, the story of Stalin's terror could be told—at least in part.

In 1962, Khrushchev approved the publication of Alexander Solzhenitsyn's dismal account of life in the gulags. *One Day in the Life of Ivan Denisovich* exposed the horrors of the prison camps for all to see.

But a little bit of openness did not mean that democracy had come to the Soviet Union. The

Communist Party continued to limit freedom of speech and democracy at home and abroad. Its tanks and soldiers crushed anti-Communist rebellions in Hungary and Czechoslovakia. Solzhenitsyn was eventually arrested for his writings and labeled an "enemy of the state." He was deported from the Soviet Union in 1974.

The empire that Stalin had built began to dissolve in 1989, when East European countries claimed their independence. In 1991, the Communist Party of the Soviet Union was forced to give up its monopoly on power. Ukraine, Belorussia, Georgia, Armenia, the Baltic states, and other republics broke away. The USSR ceased to exist. A shaky form of democracy and free-market capitalism took root in the new Russian Federation.

The breakup of the Soviet Union has made some Russians nostalgic for Stalin's empire. In little more than 20 years, his brutal rule transformed an underdeveloped country into a nuclear superpower. It turned a nation of illiterate peasants into an educated people. His leadership helped to defeat Hitler, another monstrous tyrant.

The Soviet people, however, paid an incalculable price in lives and suffering to satisfy their dictator's obsessions. During Stalin's three decades in power, at least one million people were executed. Three million died of starvation. Another million or more died from forced labor. And many millions lost years of their lives in the gulags.

These are only the victims whose fates have been documented. It may well be that many millions more were murdered during Stalin's brutal regime.

TIMELINE OF TERROR

1878

December 6, 1878: Joseph Stalin is born in the Russian territory of Georgia.

1899: Stalin is expelled from seminary and begins agitating for a communist revolution in Russia.

1905: People across Russia protest against the tsar's government.

1906–1914: Stalin organizes a gang of revolutionaries to steal money for Lenin's Bolsheviks. Stalin is arrested several times.

1914: World War I begins.

1917: The Russian Revolution succeeds in ousting the tsar. Lenin, Stalin, and other revolutionary leaders set up a Communist government.

1921: The Red Army declares victory in the Russian civil war, giving the Communists full control of the country.

1924: Lenin dies and Stalin begins to take control of the Communist Party.

1928: Stalin launches his first Five-Year Plan to turn the Soviet Union into an industrial power.

1932–33: Stalin's economic policies create a massive famine in Soviet agricultural areas.

1937–38: Stalin launches the Great Terror, imprisoning or executing nearly two million people.

1941–1945: Soviet troops fight off a German invasion during World War II; 26 million Soviet people die during the war.

1945–1948: Soviets impose Communist governments on Eastern Europe as the Cold War begins.

1953: Stalin dies at the age of 74.

1953

Glossary

apprehension (ap-ri-HEN-shen) *noun* suspicion or fear that something bad will happen

assassination (uh-sass-ih-NAY-shun) *noun* the murder of a well-known or important person

Bolsheviks (BOHL-shuh-viks) *noun* Russian Marxists who established the Communist Soviet Union after the Russian tsar was overthrown in 1917

capitalists (KAP-uh-tuh-lists) *noun* as defined by Karl Marx, the people of a society who own the businesses, factories, and land

Cheka (CHAY-kuh) *noun* the security organization that Lenin formed to hunt down political opponents of Soviet regime

collectivization (kuh-lek-tuh-vi-ZAY-shun) *noun* during Stalin's regime, the process of forcing farmers onto huge collective farms run by the government

commissar (KAM-ih-sar) *noun* until 1946, the head of a government department in the USSR

communism (KOM-yuh-niz-uhm) *noun* a system in which the government owns all land and property and controls the economic and political lives of its citizens

Communist (KOM-yuh-nist) *noun* a person supporting the Communist Party of the Soviet Union, China, or another Communist country

confiscate (KON-fih-skayt) *verb* to seize someone's property or possessions

counter-revolutionary (KOUN-tur-rev-uh-LOO-shuhn-air-ee) *noun* in the Soviet Union, a person who opposed the changes brought about by the Communist Party after the Russian Revolution

dacha (DAH-chah) *noun* a Russian country house, usually used in summer

democracy (duh-MAHK-ruh-see) *noun* a system of government in which the people hold the power, either directly or by voting to elect representatives

deport (dee-PORT) *verb* the expel someone from his or her homeland

depose (di-POSE) *verb* to forcefully remove from office

Duma (DOO-muh) *noun* the legislative body in Russia between 1906 and 1917

exile (EG-zile) *noun* the state of being kicked out of one's homeland

famine (FAM-uhn) *noun* a serious and widespread lack of food

gulags (GOO-lahgz) *noun* labor camps in the Soviet Union from 1930 to 1955 illiterate (il-LIT-ur-it) *adjective* not able to read or write

kolkhoz (kahl-KAWZ) *noun* a collective farm in the Soviet Union

kulak (KOO-lack) *noun* in the Soviet Union, a class of peasants who were considered slightly better off than other peasants; they were persecuted during collectivization

manifesto (man-ih-FEH-stoh) *noun* a public declaration of principles

Marxism (MARK-siz-im) *noun* the political and economic theories of Karl Marx; Marx predicted that capitalism would be replaced by a classless society

Okhrana (oh-KRAHN-uh) *noun* the secret police of tsarist Russia in the late 1800s and early 1900s

paranoid (PAIR-uh-noyd) *adjective* irrationally suspicious

parliament (PAR-luh-muhnt) *noun* an assembly of elected representatives who make the laws in some countries

provisional (pruh-VIZH-uh-nuhl) *adjective* temporary or interim

purge (PURJ) *noun* the removal or elimination of members of a group who are perceived to be disloyal

radical (RAD-i-kuhl) *adjective* advocating extreme political change

revolutionary (rev-uh-LOO-shuhn-air-ee) *noun* a person who supports the overthrow of his or her government

Russian Orthodox (RUHSH-in OR-thuh-doks) *adjective* describing the major church of Christianity in Russia

saboteur (sab-uh-TUR) *noun* someone who deliberately damages or destroys property to hinder the enemy's war efforts

sadistic (suh-DIS-tik) *adjective* taking pleasure from hurting others

smallpox (SMAWL-poks) *noun* a serious, very contagious disease that causes high fever and skin eruptions that can leave permanent scars

soviet (SOH-vee-et) *noun* an elected council of workers

tsar (ZAR) *noun* the emperor of Russia before the Revolution of 1917

tundra (TUHN-druh) *noun* land near the Arctic Circle where there are no trees and the ground is permanently frozen

tyrannical (tye-RAN-ih-kuhl) *adjective* ruling others in a cruel or unjust way

vigilante (vih-jih-LAN-tay) *adjective* describing a self-appointed group of citizens who take law enforcement into their own hands, without legal authority

FIND OUT MORE

Here are some books and websites with more information about
Joseph Stalin and his times.

BOOKS

Cunningham, Kevin. **Joseph Stalin and the Soviet Union (World Leaders)**. Greensboro, NC:
Morgan Reynolds, 2006. (208 pages) *A solid biography of Stalin.*

Gottfried, Ted. **The Cold War: The Rise and Fall of the Soviet Union**. Brookfield, CT:
Twenty-First Century Books, 2003. (160 pages) *Focuses on Soviet history from the end of
World War II until the end of the Cold War.*

Gottfried, Ted. **The Road to Communism**. Brookfield, CT: Twenty-First Century Books, 2002.
(144 pages) *Describes the events leading up the Russian Revolution.*

Gottfried, Ted. **The Stalinist Empire**. Brookfield, CT: Twenty-First Century Books, 2002. (128
pages) *Covers Soviet history from 1917 to World War II.*

Lugovskaya, Nina. **I Want to Live: The Diary of a Young Girl in Stalin's Russia**. New York:
Houghton Mifflin, 2006. (304 pages) *Discovered in the NKVD archives, this is the actual
diary of a teenager who survived a Stalin-era gulag.*

Rogers, Stillman. **Russia (Enchantment of the World, Second Series)**. New York: Children's
Press, 2002. (144 pages) *Describes the history, geography, and people of Russia.*

Solzhenitsyn, Alexander. **One Day in the Life of Ivan Denisovich**. New York: Signet Classics,
2008 (151 pages). *This powerful novel, which describes a typical day for an inmate at a Stalinist
labor camp, is based on Solzhenitsyn's own experiences.*

WEBSITES

http://encarta.msn.com/encyclopedia_761559200/stalin.html *MSN Encarta's online
encyclopedia article on Joseph Stalin.*

http://www.pbs.org/behindcloseddoors *The online companion to the PBS series*
World War II: Behind Closed Doors, *a detailed look at the relationship between the
Allied leaders Stalin, Franklin Roosevelt, and Churchill.*

http://www.fordham.edu/halsall/mod/modsbook39.html *This page on the Russian
Revolution, from Fordham University's Internet Modern History Sourcebook, includes
links to resources on Joseph Stalin and Stalinism.*

INDEX

AUTHOR'S NOTE AND BIBLIOGRAPHY

In 1983, I traveled across much of the Soviet Union, from Leningrad in the north to Tbilisi in the south. At the time it was inconceivable that anything could loosen the Communist Party's hold on Russia and the other republics of the USSR. Yet less than ten years later, the empire imploded. Its former citizens—from political scientists to school kids—struggled to make sense of how their country had self-destructed.

In the aftermath, historians were gradually allowed to burrow into the archives of Stalin's rule. They discovered documents that revealed the dictator's use of terror to manipulate virtually every aspect of life in his country.

But even with his cruelty exposed, Stalin's popularity seems to be making a comeback. In a recent opinion poll, he won approval from 47 percent of Russians.

Why do so many people still favor Stalin while Hitler, another of history's most destructive tyrants, is widely despised? One reason may be that unlike the Nazis, Stalin and his henchmen were never forced to account for their crimes.

The following sources have proved most helpful in researching this book.

Conquest, Robert. **The Harvest of Sorrow: Soviet Collectivization and the Terror-Famine**. New York: Oxford University Press, 1986.

Davies, Sarah and James Harris, editors. **Stalin: A New History**. New York: Cambridge University Press, 2005.

Goldman, Wendy Z. **Terror and Democracy in the Age of Stalin**. New York: Cambridge University Press, 2007.

Lewis, Jonathan and Phillip Whitehead. **Stalin: A Time for Judgement**. New York: Pantheon Books, 1990.

Medvedev, Roy and Zhores Medvedev. **The Unknown Stalin: His Life, Death, and Legacy**. New York: The Overlook Press, 2003.

Montefiore, Simon Sebag. **Stalin: The Court of the Red Tsar**. New York: Vintage Books, 2005.

Montefiore, Simon Sebag. **Young Stalin**. New York: Vintage Books, 2007.

Rayfield, Donald. **Stalin and His Hangmen**. New York: Random House, 2004.

Service, Robert. **Stalin: A Biography**. Cambridge, MA: Harvard University Press, 2005.

—Sean McCollum